ABOUT VERVE POETRY FESTIVAL

VERVE isn't your typical literary festival. Still only seven years old, it has already made a huge mark on the national poetry scene, noted for its:
   Roof-shaking spoken word sets
   Readings and workshops by award-winning poets
   Boundary-pushing poetry/theatre performances
   Lively children's events
   and much, much more!
Most importantly, VERVE is a festival for everyone to enjoy poetry together - where performance poets and page poets mingle and appreciate each other's art, where experimental poets swap numbers with children's poets. VERVE is for beginners and seasoned poetry afficiandos and everything in between. What ever kind of poet or poetry fan you are, no-one gets left out at VERVE!

http://vervepoetryfestival.com
enquiries@vervepoetryfestival.com

A Gift, Once Given, Must Not Be Spurned

The Verve Anthology of Eco-Poetry

BIRMINGHAM

PUBLISHED BY VERVE POETRY PRESS
https://vervepoetrypress.com
mail@vervepoetrypress.com

All rights reserved
© 2024 all individual authors

The right of all individuals to be identified as author if this work has been asserted in accordance with section 77 of the Copyright, Designs and Patents Act 1988.

No part of this work may be reproduced, stored or transmitted in any form or by any means, graphic, electronic, recorded or mechanical, without the prior written permission of the publisher.

FIRST PUBLISHED FEB 2024

Printed and bound in the UK
by Imprint Digital, Exeter

ISBN: 978-1-913917-49-4

CONTENTS

Introduction by Helen Mort

Unst - *Alison Tanik*	19
the sun never gets sick or wakes up late or smokes too much - *Oli Isaac*	21
Charm for Unfruitful Land - *Milena Williamson*	22
We're on a Cliff Edge - *Evie Williams*	23
Saving the little things - *Disha Ramesh*	24
Eel - *Ben Verinder*	26
Prayer That My Body Makes Good Compost - *Timothy Kiely*	27
Byrdie - *Sue Spiers*	28
The Skylark's First Flight - *Emily Hunt*	29
Among us Lives a Little Bird - *Aneesha Sandhu*	31
Ἀγάπη, or How Caves Love You - *Sophia Argyris*	33
A Psalm For Plastic - *Roger Hare*	35
Storm - *Lesley Quayle*	38
Not for the Online Followers - *Japmeh Kaur Gujral*	39
To the children of my land - *Lilly Prince*	41
Before the Floods - *Hannah Burrows*	43

An increasing incidence of extreme weather events - *Tom Sastry*	44
The day after, watching a kingfisher - *Harry Slater*	45
The tick of the clock - *Laurie Wiseman*	46
Eco-Problem - *Kai Lee*	47
A prayer for the future child - *Rachit Sharma*	49
Naming his daughter - *Lily Dyu*	51
Crocuses, etc. - *Elizabeth Gibson*	53
Songbird Without Song - *Isabelle Wei*	54
Sickness in a Cool, Coastal Wood - *Dominic Anaya Gulaya*	56
On the rocks - *Corinna Broad*	57
Calima - *Isabella Mead*	58
Fruit pickers, south of Rome - *Caroline Maldonado*	59
Emergency Oxygen - *Agata Maslowska*	60
On Precipitation - *Ger Duffy*	62

Poet Biographies

In Praise of Overthinking by Helen Mort

I write in praise of overthinking. In a world of snap decisions and juggernaut progress, it's our chance to slow things down. Let's do more: more productive worrying, more creative troublemaking, more halting, stopping, thinking more-than-twice. As poets, we're already ahead of the curve here. We're always making difficulties for ourselves, getting stuck on definitions, implied meanings, paradoxes within our language. We rarely let a term go uninterrogated.

Take the idea of an 'eco-poetry competition'. Before I can even begin to contemplate the honour of judging such a prize (thank you, Verve!), I'm hung up on the phrase's constituent parts. What does it mean for poems to 'compete' against one another? I like the idea of poems teeming and swarming, setting each other off, egging each other on. I'm less keen on the idea of them jostling for position, elbowing each other in the hope of getting my highly subjective approval.

Once we've dismissed the idea that any work of art can be 'best', once we see competition as an invitation to participate, an opportunity for future dialogue, then I'm interested again. I read every single poem submitted for this prize several times in detail and each piece offered a challenge to my thinking. My favourites were the pieces I couldn't forget after I had finished reading them. If you like them, they might validate or inspire your own thinking. If you don't like them, they might encourage you to write something in response. 'Competition' can generate a healthy dialogue.

But what about 'eco-poetry'? That's a far bigger can of worms (the anthropocentrism inherent in an image of worms in a can isn't lost on me either). How do we get the balance between 'eco' and poetic'? Should we even think about balance in a woefully unbalanced environmental context? As someone who has always written about landscape, particularly the gritstone-rich moorlands around Sheffield and Derbyshire where I grew up, I once thought that all poetry about nature was inherently environmental. I thought that to honour something with your attention is to make an argument for its continued existence. By writing about places I loved, I was preserving them. Now, I think that's only part of the challenge.

I'm sure my favourite poet, the late, great Norman MacCaig, would have laughed at my youthful naivety. He was always alert to the hypocrisy of the nature writer, the traps we so easily fall into. He wanted to evoke animals and habitats on their own terms: the 'goatishness' of goat, herons 'wrapped in heron', a glacier which couldn't possibly be likened to anything human or human-made. As he put it:

> 'I loathe the pathetic fallacy. Makes it rain when you feel sad; makes it sunny when you feel gay. I loathe burdening outside objects with human feelings, making them some kind of sympathetic translator of my own tiny small self. I hate it.'

There wasn't even a hint of the pathetic fallacy in the entries I read for the Verve competition. MacCaig's stridency was honoured. (ASIDE: I don't trust poets who aren't slightly contradictory though: it always pleases me to note how brilliant MacCaig is at crafting images that compare animals to aspects of the world as seen / built by humans, like in his poem 'Movements').

Trying to define the 'eco-poem' in a piece for the Poetry Foundation, Jon Shoptaw observes:

> '...an ecopoem needs to be environmental and it needs to be environmentalist. By environmental, I mean first

that an ecopoem needs to be about the nonhuman natural world — wholly or partly, in some way or other, but really and not just figuratively. In other words, an ecopoem is a kind of nature poem. But an ecopoem needs more than the vocabulary of nature.'

What does that ineffable 'more' mean in practice though? Shoptaw elaborates:

'... an ecopoem is environmental is that it is ecocentric, not anthropocentric. Human interests cannot be the be-all and end-all of an ecopoem.'

When I was judging the varied pieces of writing entered for this year's competition, I felt I could identify that 'more' when I saw it. Or rather I knew it when I felt it – good poems have a visceral effect.

The entries for the 11-17 competition filled me with hope: they were characterised by discontent but also a call to action. They indicated a group of new creative writers who aren't prepared to settle for the world we've given them. Young writers took on topics like biodiversity loss, 'natural' disasters caused by the unnatural and the extent to which we live our lives online. Birds were a striking motif, a desire to see the planet from above. It was exciting to see many of the poets working with rhyme and form, carefully considering the impact of stanza and line breaks.

In the adult category, the poems that made it onto my shortlist and into my 'top' selection (I can hear the poems tutting at my reductive language) all had an angle that I found interesting or surprising: one notable example was a psalm to plastic ('where shall I go from you, darling polymer?'), relentless in its rhythm. There were countless startling wake-up calls, like the conclusion of 'Emergency Oxygen':

Even the emergency oxygen
falling from the panels
above our heads
won't make us last...

There was a poem about rain which scattered itself across the page as droplets ('On Precipitation'), form evoking strange and observable patterns (and broken patterns) in the weather. There was 'Storm;' which perfectly held human and wild elements in tension: 'I worried about the storm. It worried the house....'. These days, our British tradition of constantly talking about the weather has a political urgency. In 'An increasing incidence of extreme weather events' the poet had created an apocalyptic, dystopian but very familiar sounding future, fear and the evacuation of houses:

The police told us to leave
for the nowhere we had to go
in the nothing we had to get there...

As well as an awareness of peril, there was light in the selection I chose too, a sense of reprieve. 'Crocuses etc' begins:

Tonight, the wind is no longer pain-cold-full-of-grit,
but is instead a tongue, a vast creature greeting us,
curling and testing....

It ends with the narrator musing that they should keep their 'heart petals open'.

Yes, there were many moments of conventional (and unconventional) nature-descriptive writing which impressed me with their acuity. But the poems I loved always took this further. 'On the rocks' lulled me into a false sense of security – I'm free from climate anxiety! I'm having a pleasant drink in a bar! But wait, even the glass contains a 'miniature Arctic': 'The ice cube is a glacier / somewhere in Svalbard....'.

Or take the opening sections of 'The day after, watching a kingfisher'. The bird is first described in all its resplendent colour:

A liquid flicker of teal and copper
Like polished glass
A shimmering blade
A retreating flare

So far so good. So far so beautiful. But then the bird becomes:

The colour of the pen he used
to mark the point the water reached
up the plaster in the stone house
Ten years,
three in four.
Are we pretending we're not standing
up to our knees in river?

I was unable to get that searching question out of my head. The poems on my highly-commended list were all through with pretence. They dealt in realties. And they dared to think beyond those paradigms too. There was the wonderfully titled 'Charm for Unfruitful Land' with its stark, darkly comic opening: 'The good news is the wolves have returned to Europe. /The bad news is people are killing wolves again.' There was the strangely hopeful tone of 'Prayer that my body makes good compost', imagining the narrator's decomposition and return to a world 'where everything is in readiness, / all eaten, all uncovered, / all sent out and all recovered.'

Thinking about the more-than-human, the pre-and-post-human doesn't mean that we exclude people from our poems. On the contrary, these entries which I particularly admired were rich and varied in the ways they charted the impact of climate emergency on the world's population. This was perhaps most apparent in pieces like 'Fruit pickers, south of Rome' and its harrowing 'days of thirst', or the haunting 'Calima', where sudden weather makes everything seem dusted in a film of 'dessicated blood'. Some of the pieces mourned a loss of innocence in the speakers somehow, like the taut stanzas of 'Before the Floods' which recalled how the protagonists once felt 'untouchable as frost before morning break'. The poems I loved raised questions about positionality and who has been writing about the natural world and for whom. 'Naming His Daughter' is a tour-de-force of a poem which interrogates the power inherent in naming:

> I remember a talk I gave, a man asked me,
> *Why aren't there more people of colour in the outdoors?*

We are left to wonder who should be responsible for answering that question, thinking about the burden placed on the speaker. So the poems I admired were whipsmart when it came to human-and-human relations too and how they fit into the web of eco-poetry. In 'Unst', the narrator realises that they are not at the centre of things, even as they sit immersed in June chill, between 'a copper-chalk sky and the wet sand':

...I realised for the first time we didn't belong,
that the earth was tilting for its own pleasure,
and didn't even know we were waiting.

I haven't finished remarking on the commended poems yet, but I want to take a few moments to explore what drew me to my three winners (poems tutting again at my proprietorial language – what makes them 'yours', Helen?).

I liked 'How Caves Love You', awarded third place, because it was so strange and compelling, so tender. It opens:

I always thought caves would taste of stone, of echo
and how light loves the edges of their mouths.

Let's spend a moment unpicking that stanza and its subtle dance with the more-than-human. You could think there's anthropocentrism at play here in that extraordinary image 'light loves the edges of their mouths' but there's much more going on (and besides, this isn't personification bingo), both in the notion of interplay between light and cave being wholly benign but also in the destabilising of presumed knowledge: if the speaker 'always thought' something, presumably they are about to be proved wrong. So it goes. And we have our own ideas challenged too. Caves are not possessive. There are subtle lessons here for us, in the fact of being wholly open:

In our clutching world to be so agape is terrifying.
Agape, so close to the Greek word for love.

This is a gentle, fierce poem. I'd go as far as to call it a kind of pan-psychic love poem (now there's a phrase I didn't imagine writing.)

In second place, 'Eel' was the kind of poem I could read a hundred times and find something new in it with each successive reading. It purports to offer 'stories of resurrection' but what follows in numbered sections is far more profoundly slippery (sorry). It is a difficult poem to paraphrase – to appreciate it, you really do just have to read it. Ideally at least ten times. That's true of all pieces of creative writing of course but especially this disjointed but wholly convincing creature. I don't want to spoil the ending for you, but there's a delightful shock, a sense that resurrection is also terrifying. The speaker's assertion that 'for an angel I would employ the eel' is justified, but in a way that holds the stench 'of death'.

The poem that rose to the surface as my winner has an enviably great title: 'the sun never gets sick or wakes up late or smokes too much'. It sounds as if it is going to be arch, tricksy even. And it does bristle with dark humour: 'we lay on your front lawn persuading our shadows / to stand up' (what a fantastic line break, incidentally / not incidentally).

But there's more at play here, disguised by the lack of capitalisation and staccato statements: '...you joke that the sun could go / on a killing spree and it would blame us / for having high expectations.' In the age of climate emergency, a joke is never just a joke.

The speaker worries that the earth's rotation will come to a halt and, again, their arch pronouncement seems prophetic. It is a piece which comments on the apathy we can feel in the face of global warming and global disaster, the way it can be hard to know where to begin (but we must).

I think what I loved most about this poem – apart from its refusal to take itself too seriously somehow, even given the gravity of its subject – was its last word on the capacity we have as humans for self-delusion. It's there in the final line: 'our accelerated mortality gives me back my appetite.'

So the various commended and winning entries did all I could have hoped for: made me laugh, made me grieve, terrified me and made me hope. MacCaig wouldn't be happy unless I singled out a poem in praise of creatures and luckily there were many wonderful pieces that tried to grapple with the consciousness of other beings. My favourite of these was 'Byrdie', a poem celebrating the brilliance of the ingenious octopus:

I love her YouTube clips
  where the keeper puts a crab in a container
to watch a fistful of arms
twist off a lid
  or squeeze through an impossible gap
    to midden the feast....

It made me think of a spine-chilling story a good friend once told me (and which I'm now going to repeat, unprovoked, with a violence-against-sea-creatures trigger warning). One of those anecdotes that tempts you to arrogantly think 'I'll write about that', only to be defeated by the surreal facts of the case which resist fictionalising. It was about her father travelling to an international business event where there was a dinner which promised to serve live octopus. To his horror, a still-moving creature was carried out on a platter, the intention being to slice slivers from its tentacles at the table.

The plot twist was that the octopus got up from its plate and scuttled for the door, making a run for it. I wish the tale had a happy ending. But because it involves people, I'm afraid it doesn't: the escape artist was apprehended, consigned to its original fate. That story always haunted me, filled me with a singular sense of misery. It seemed like a depressing metaphor for what we've done and are doing to the planet with each consecutive failure of action and imagination. But while poetry might only have a tangential connection to the former, it can certainly help with the latter. And action begins with imagination, after all. In poetry, we can create another version where the octopus sneaks out of the door and finds an unlikely way back to the sea. Or, even better, turns the tables on its captors and waves a knife at them instead. You pick your version: Tarantino or standard. Now get out there and write the poem. We're counting on you.

Link:
https://www.poetryfoundation.org/poetrymagazine/articles/70299/why-ecopoetry

ABOUT HELEN MORT:

Helen Mort is a poet and novelist. Her collections *Division Street* (2013), *No Map Could Show Them* (2016) and *The Illustrated Woman* (2022) are all published by Chatto & Windus. She's a Fellow of the Royal Society of Literature and teaches at Manchester Metropolitan University. She lives in Sheffield.

Helen appeared at the first ever VERVE Festival in 2017, and appeared again last year (2023) when she headlined alongside Imtiaz Dharker and Hannah Sullivan. She also workshopped at the festival both for adults and for young poets in association with Poetry Society Young Poets Network and took part in our first ever Zoom season of fortnightly workshops which ran June through to November 2023.

A Gift, Once Given, Must Not Be Spurned

Unst
Alison Tanik

that time,

on the island for solstice,
with the world tilting drunk on its axis,
and the rain lying flat on its back in the milky gloam,
tilting with it,
yet still coming up under my hood,
to nip in short, sharp gasps at my face.

we sat on Skew, in the whitewash gap,
cast between a copper-chalk sky and the wet sand,
soaked and cold; our hands, pink sea anemones,
raw in the June chill, clutching half-empty cans,
all promise of their joy lost
somewhere between cornershop and beach.

greedily, we waited for the simmer dim,
the midnight sun, slim circles of eucharist bread
to sit on both horizons -
as if the world owed it to us:
our bodies unclocked and unsprung
from too-long days and too-short nights,
our limbs stiff from the damp
and the heft of the slate landscape.

and, it was then, that summer, on Unst,
in the dusk,
with the hours becoming muted shadows,
that I realised for the first time we didn't belong,
that the earth was tilting for its own pleasure,
and didn't even know we were waiting.

the sun never gets sick or wakes up late or smokes too much
Oli Isaac (!st Place)

we refuse to believe the sun rises earlier every day
to only reach its highest point at noon. since it gets harder and harder

to get up and give people something
to rely on. we lay on your front lawn persuading our shadows

to stand up to the sun. you joke that the sun could go
on a killing spree and it would blame us

for having high expectations. there is a point
when sunsets and sunrises look the same in photos. i worry

the earth's rotation will come to a halt
because it forgot why it was doing it in the first place—

stuck. half-set. embarrassed
the weather doesn't change and no-one sleeps. its most beautiful

moment fading into a mundane sight that kills us all.
our accelerated mortality gives me back my appetite.

Charm for Unfruitful Land
Milena Williamson

The good news is the wolves have returned to Europe. The bad news is people are killing wolves again. I own no underwear from this island. There is no purely wild place left on this island. I buy wildflower seeds from the dark web. I walk on the earth while there is still time and sprinkle seeds on river banks, lawns and graveyards. The smoke pours across the border, becoming sky. It's time to buy an air filter and give it a name. I am living inside a well and high above me, the bucket framed against the sky is Europe. We have drilled into Antarctica to find the most transparent ice. This ice is compressed by other ice which means it is very dark down there, dark enough to see neutrinos belly-flop into light. We are living in the overlap. We can seed clouds from seawater.

We're on a Cliff Edge
Evie Williams (11)

Picture a place where animals roam free
on land, and under the sea.
Where computers and phones were never a thing,
And where winter would peacefully turn into spring.

Now, picture plastic all over this dream land,
this isn't a picture any more, need to take a stand.
150 species die day by day,
This wonderland is now black and grey.

The people in power need to hear,
if we don't act now, consequences will appear.
Generations won't see the beauty of all the green,
instead, they'll see this world through a screen.

Come on people, stop this parallel universe that's coming ever so quick,
we're on a cliff edge, don't let the clock tick.

Saving the little things
Disha Ramesh (12)

When you actually think about the earth
You're all like, oh Mother Nature
Save the planet!
Climate change is bad

Well, it is
But when I think of the Earth
I don't think about the 'issues' of the Earth
Don't get me wrong
I love the world
We live on it!

I think about the little things,
When you accidentally drop a tin can in the paper bin?
When you throw that one sweet wrapper on the ground
Okay maybe that was a bit too specific

I think about the 'me' issues
I didn't expect you to understand
See I think about what I've done
Like spiders
Everyone has killed a spider once in their lifetime
If you haven't well
You're the chosen one

Anyway, back to topic
Yeah I'm not exactly eco friendly myself
But not everybody is
But unlike them I'm trying
You know , to be eco friendly

Being eco friendly isn't just about saving the planet,
it's about saving the little things
Just one person can make a difference
Unfortunately, I can't do it alone
So join me
Join me in saving the little things
(And the planet of course)

Eel
Ben Verinder (2nd Place)

[1] These are stories of resurrection:

[2] Rajendra Singh cut 376 johads in the death bed of the Arvari and it sprang back to life;

[3] Old Father Thames was woken out of sleep though he stank of death. So too the Don, Varattar, Mersey.

[4] And for an angel I would employ the eel, it being metamorphic and of three ranks.

[5] First glass then yellow then silver, of two domains (fresh and salt-water) and unable to commit a sin.

[6] A strong climber, itself capable of revival.

[7] This I have seen: my grandmother bent over the cottage sink to wash the eels we caught and bludgeoned at Little Beck.

[8] How the water shocked them back to life.

[9] How her scream sounded like the opening of a tomb.

Prayer That My Body Makes Good Compost
Timothy Kiely

That when my cheeks come to know the kiss
of gravel and moss; when the brown mouth opens,
I will find that root and rhizome
and the musk of rot and the rolling pressure

of time and water are all utterly
familiar; that nothing of this
is alien, nothing final, just
the endless work and churn and emerging

and folding into passage and this –
where everything is in readiness,
all eaten, all uncovered,
all sent out and all recovered.

That the want is always in me
for waking in the dark, my head
alive with the bells of worms and rootlets
stirring underneath the slaughter,

pushing up to see a singular sun,
knowing that I had not been refused.
That even where we drop, new worlds
will burst out. That earth turns.

Byrdie
Sue Spiers

Octopus vulgaris

    I love her YouTube clips
  where the keeper puts a crab in a container
to watch a fistful of arms
twist off a lid
  or squeeze through an impossible gap
    to midden the feast.

    I love her russet blush,
  angry with her keeper's ruse and finds
a stone
rolled in prawn guts
  she thought was food
    but less tasty than dead coral.

    I love her asymmetry;
  arms in pairs and independently waving
each curled
in suckerly whorls,
  thick to clamber,
    thinned into tendrils to probe.

    I love her ink swirling
  through brine,
the jet of propulsion she throws to escape.
Even a shark-bite
  doesn't leave her oddly limbed.
    She regrows.

The Skylark's First Flight
Emily Hunt (17)

What our hearts needed was this -

so we listened, we waited
for the first to rouse the landscape
with song, to become the sky
to rise on invisible columns
warbling, disappearing,
climbing, free-falling
even though it was winter
even though we were numb.
We shielded our eyes
searched for them
in the strengthening light

and the season turned - we saw seedlings rise
charmed like snakes by flute and whistle
fields turn from barren to green
shoots push through the expectant earth
and the crop grew dense around their nests
covered them, swaddled them
this year's young woven into sculpted cups
but we knew as we walked among
the static blades that one would
give itself away - rustle its way
out and up, elevate us with its serenade
and summer days brought
cracking clay and gorse pods
splitting on the hill, as jackdaws
tumbled into sunsets

and we hoped they had fledged
when harvest came, the ground quaked
and dust rose thick as mist.
Such potential at our mercy
promise shattered by machinery -
but we waited, and walked
through all those songless months
hoping the next generation would rise,
carry us in its flight.

Among us Lives a Little Bird
Aneesha Sandhu (13)

Go little bird fly,

fly high soar

to the sky.

Fly, fly little bird

past the burning trees

past the skyscrapers

trying to pierce your wings.

Fly high.

Little bird spread your wings

fly far away from home

because little bird ...

They want wood.

Little Bird

the sky is filling with gas

smoke and ash

don't fly too high

you'll die little bird.

Would your children believe

the sky used to be blue?

Little bird

take no notice.

Little bird fly

Fly past the oil
rig draining your home.

Don't make a peep little bird, they will drain you too.

Oh little bird watch your planet die.

Watch those who kill it blissfully unaware

of your existence.

Unaware

that it's your world too.

Fly high little bird

Please

Don't cry

Αγάπη, or How Caves Love You
Sophia Argyris (3rd Place)

I always thought caves would taste of stone, of echo
and how light loves the edges of their mouths.

I don't think of them as possessive. Tides come and go
exhaling their fish and seaweed breath, bats hang out

and leave again. If creatures choose to live within such
cavernous lungs, become eyeless and pale over centuries,

caves accept it all. If something dies within their walls
they will cradle the body as it dwindles to bone,

because a gift, once given, must not be spurned.
Caves don't understand time, but as they age

gypsum flowers and rimstone dams may form
in their veins. Their hearts are always wide open.

In our clutching world to be so agape is terrifying.
Agape, so close to the Greek word for love.

I thought I knew them through my fear of dark
and the pressing weight of rock, how it curves

like a petrified sky. But last time I stepped
inside the earth, its throat was not as I'd thought.

I sat in pitching shadow, all light extinguished,
listening to the booming silence. I took a pinch

of darkness between my fingers and let it dissolve
on my tongue. It didn't taste of anything expected.

It was powder from the wing of a day flying moth.
It was the opposite of lonely.

[Αγάπη: Agapi, meaning empathetic or universal love in Greek)

A Psalm For Plastic
Roger Hare

After Psalm 139 (The Bible)

O Plastic, you search me and know me!
You are there at my sitting and rising;
    are acquainted
    with all my ways.

Where shall I go from you, darling polymer?
If I ascend the Himalayas
    you are there, your slender fragments
    clutched in feathers of fallen snow.

If I descend to the deepest trench
    of the deepest ocean,
    you are there, sedimenting
    with mud and morbid ooze.

Pelagic, you set sail – your water music
    enters flesh and fluid of everything
    in the sea that beats.

Inland, you are there in marsh, stream,
    pool, and lake: make
    rivers arterial for your passage.

Above the waterline, your quietest notes
    fill the score
    of all our indrawn breaths,
    take placental seats at our budding

and after birth, are fed
        to each little let-it-be
    unwittingly, in breast milk
    laced with your supplement.

In partition days of pandemic you were there
        to divide our breath,
    secure us from herd mentality – how
    we clasped you, then dashed you
    to the ground.

Where shall I go from you, darling polymer?
Your symphony of descending chords
        searches soil, tests its depth,
    traces all its spaces with beads and threads.

In darkness and in light you're there –
        decorate the world
    with no care for who you catch or tangle,
    what views you jangle with your
    unfashionable veils:

I once looked up to see you
        wrap an angel of yourself
    around the aerial of a cottage
    in one of England's prettiest towns.

Where shall I go from you, darling polymer?
I can rise on the wings of the day,
    shelter in the silk of space,
        sample the ice that tips our north and south
            and still find your resistant flour.

You hem me in, behind and before,
and lay your hand upon me
but listen to prophecy held
    in the heart of seeds:

when ash has turned to ash
    and been raised-up again,
when ice has come and gone,
when plastic is a memory
    held in rock,
what's woven from the earth will fly
    and we, we will have to learn again
    the art of fire.

Italicised quote from Psalm 139 v 5 The Bible,
English Standard Version (2002 Publisher:HarperCollins)

Storm
Lesley Quayle

I worried about the storm. It worried the house,
harried the ash trees until they shed their brittle bones
across grass, crushing heroic daffodils
in their small mime of sunshine.

The map had changed by morning,
and the shape of land, altered by wind
and water, lay suddenly unrecorded, masked
by floods, ruptured by the gale.

This winter has been soft till now
and, unwary, we forgot how it can rise,
malevolent and vicious, more powerful
than us, with its keen teeth bared.

Come spring, there will be fewer greens,
even inland the colour will be diminished,
and freckled cattle, used to parasol oaks
and willows, will have to bear the red sun,
unremitting, on their backs.

Not for the Online Followers
Japmeh Kaur Gujral (12)

Amid the ceaseless hum of screens,
We seek the truth...
In the tangled web of ones and zeroes we're caught,
Real beauty not pixels, but nature's living proof.

With the forest's ancient wisdom,
Why do we need the search bar?
The babbling brook with its crystal-clear song,
Why do we yearn for the online streamings flow?

Regal mountains, their heads held high,
We glimpse at them through the white light of screens.
Deserts, waiting patiently in the candescent sun,
We see them in images on a glowing interface.

Meadows bloom, with copious colours,
Shared on social media, for likes to breed.
Fields, where a sea of viridescent stretches to the horizon,
Edited and played with for the followers.

Sunrises and sunsets paint the sky with stories,
We're only lucky if we can find an aesthetic 'pic' online.
Stars in the night sky shine like precious beacons,
Can we find a perfect picture of them for a phone background?

Hola
Willkommen
Go; travel the world, and see for yourself the Seven Wonders,
Not just on a vlog.

"Come play with me!" Mother Nature says.
"And not by polluting me with fireworks!"
"Where have all the children gone?"
"Stuck to screens too early on!"

But in our fake wonderland of devices galore,
We only peek at the world through a digital light.
Is it a connection we crave?
In the online streams, like sailors on a wave.

Beneath the screens enchanting glows, we always lose our sight,
But in nature's embrace we find the truth we seek.
In images we wander but truth is not bright,
Beauty isn't online; it's in real life.

To the children of my land
Lilly Prince (15)

To the children of my land
It's earth here and I'm raising a hand
being honest with all my heart and soul
spreading a message everyone should be told.

I am constantly changing,
however, don't feel like rearranging -
it's all about being fair.
I provide you with land, water and clean air
in exchange you disperse of your
disrespect and disdain elsewhere.
Why don't you even seem to care?

Habitats are dying, a loss of biodiversity is rising.
Our animals are crying. Why are you finding this surprising?
My skin of scenery now transformed.
My highest peaks eroded that once stood so tall.
A fire is lit, ripping and crippling me down to the core.
My heart is singed, and you're just stood there
watching that gore!

So let's unite, standing together -
person and planet ignited forever!
We shall embrace each other's change.
We shall protect each other in vain.
We shall not forget all of the pain.

I am your mother nature, yesterday, tomorrow and today.
Let's stay on track and never stray.
Yours sincerely, Earth.

P.S. Cherish all our memories
For they won't remain.
But in the ticking of time
We will find our way.
Because it's a journey for growth
In each passing day.

Before the Floods
Hannah Burrows

and the murk of sky descending to make a home with us—
before the breakdowns or howls of unromantic blizzards

a mass of swans sit willow-necked, a flock of questions
and the cold is cracked open by bright stabs of our laughter

we play at smoking as hot breath curls through fingers
try to trace the outline of the jetty, made stupid with youth

with nothing yet more painful than my blisters from your boots,
and nothing yet to let go of but each other, or the truth—

we were freewheeling in the backseat of your mother's car,
untouchable as frost before morning break,

made lighter than fear, this rising.

An increasing incidence of extreme weather events
Tom Sastry

We watched the charts all week
as the old hurricane's great lash
curled back across the ocean, not weakening
until we saw Bristol in its path.

The police told us to leave
for the nowhere we had to go
in the nothing we had to get there.
They would take the gloves off for looters.

Abandoned people are always crazy
like a fool who squares up to a storm.
Crazy like us, on the roofs of Easton
waving at the news helicopter

as the studio repeats the warnings
we were apparently ignoring
when we walked onto the M32
in a world already shaking and tearing

for a woman desperate to pass her child
into the mystery of a stranger's car
which was crammed to the corners
with the old necessities of home.

The day after, watching a kingfisher
Harry Slater

Twice, oil in water flash
Like a hurled gem
A liquid flicker of teal and copper
Like polished glass
A shimmering blade
A retreating flare
The colour of the pen he used
to mark the point the water reached
up the plaster in the stone house
Ten years,
three in four.
Are we pretending we're not standing
up to our knees in river?
I don't know the sound it made
hidden behind my gasp
A dress rehearsal in blue, desperate breath
You didn't see it
Like guilt resolved along contour lines

The tick of the clock
Laurie Wiseman (12)

The beat of wild horses' hooves over the moonlit moor,
the crash of sparkling waves against the edge of the shore,
all of these I treasured -
all of these I took.
The stars over a small town in the dead of night,
the blazing autumn canopy pierced by dappled light,
all of these I cherished -
all of these I snuffed.
The crunch of pristine snow under foot,
summer's haze in a chalk brook,
all of these I snatched -
all these that I loved.
But I remain.
I remain every tick of the clock, each lifetime, each aeon,
I was, I am, I will be there,
For every silenced beat of a horse's hooves over a barren moor,
At the crash of every frothing wave against the choked shore.

Eco-Problem
Kai Lee (14)

The Earth is dying slowly, and we all know it.
Our flower made of earth and sea is wilting.
The water slowing growing higher and higher,
The ozone hole slowly growing larger and larger.

We may be the disease wiping out nature,
With our motor-cars and production lines.
Or we may just be a catalyst for destruction,
Just helping a dying world die faster.
Either way, we are still contributors,
Sinking the ship that we sail.

And *so what*, we have non-profits
To save the trees and save the seas?
We balance out these efforts
With styrofoam boxes and plastic bags.
Produced over and over and over again.

At least, that's what I thought a long time ago,
But I see a future where we change our ways.
It's distant but it's a glimmering light,
And it pierces through the dark smog of the city,
Like a beacon, signalling our path to freedom.
But some are blind to the brightness.

Some people say we can't save Earth.
We have already killed our planet, and we are living on the remnants.
That we, *homo sapiens*, human beings, are a pest.
A pest that has killed Earth, and will be killed along with it.

But a pest will never change.
A cockroach will never stop infesting,
A termite will never stop eating wood,
A mouse will never stop making holes,
But man can change, so a man can't be a pest.

Some people say it's too late.
The damage is too much, and it's irreversible.

But it's *not* to late to change, it's *never* too late to change.
Each small step creates change.
Because a journey of a thousand trees starts with one seedling.
And even though one seedling may not amount to much,
It can encourage a whole forest to grow.
A forest tall and strong, so strong nothing can bother it.

You are the seedling.
You can make change, you can cause life to sprout.
So take care of the seedling,
And watch it grow into a forest.

A prayer for the future child
Rachit Sharma

and for Mt. Kenya tunneled like a scented lilac candle
its porous wick perched quiet in a sunbird's gut,

for its rivers wrung through a hose -
and its Mugumo trees standing like starving shrines,

for its raspy air setting my words into coarse song,
and for the black kites dropping in the shape of a wound,

for the woman who tells me -
that when her ancestors were being trafficked from West Africa
    to Columbia
their grandmothers' heads turned into seed banks
as they hastily braided a variety of rice seeds in their hair
setting a crown jeweled in future
"while the world was centuries away from Climatology"
- the snow of her eyes flying silver sparks,

a prayer for the tongue
disallowed,
shaved,
swallowing blood off the razor bumps,

for the ones who are taking us on unsolicited voyages to the
    moon and Mars
and for the rare few who are braiding seeds and hope and future

for the indigenous farmer from the south of Mexico who said, "the only word that's second to gratitude in our prayers, is - resistance..."

In August 2023, activists from over 20+ global south countries, working against - deepening inequalities, destruction of ecosystems, catastrophic climate change, ruptures in socio-cultural fabrics, and the violent dispossession of living beings - gathered in Nanyuki, Kenya. The gathering was hosted under the network of Global Tapestry of Alternatives - to grieve, to heal, and to envision a better world for the future child.

Naming his daughter
Lily Dyu

My father chose my Chinese name *Wai Yin*,
meaning 'sweetgrass swallow', the bird
a messenger of spring and happiness,
a symbol of good fortune and grace.

I met my first swallows after settling in Wales:
embroidering the air, diving on the brook,
gossiping on phone wires. Sojourners making
two places home, like my father who once

scanned Taishan skies for their return,
watched them skimming paddy fields, and
when he disturbed their nests, was beaten
by his mother, afraid of bringing bad luck.

Yin! he'd shout from the kitchen. *Little Swallow!
This order is ready. Sweet and sour pork.* And off I'd fly.

***

Is my name the charm that wilds my life?
The spell that conjures the thrush to sing
this morning, performing on the walnut tree?

Does my name, when called, magic the mist
of bluebells floating in the woods? Invoke
the sun's lemon light through day-old beech leaves?
And raise the drowsy bees drifting
in the apple blossom?

Or did sacrifice, not sorcery, manifest
my mountains and meadows? Your years
washing laundry pledged for river and sea,
takeaway days swapped for forest and moor?

> I remember a talk I gave, a man asked me,
> *Why aren't there more people of colour in the outdoors?*

***

A woodpecker swings on the feeder, then vanishes.
Flash of red, shy and hungry woodland guest,
this dazzling season of song and nest when gangs
of teenage bluetits crash through the garden.

The village's children once fell asleep to curlews
crying in the fields, to screaming swifts in the lane,
but now I lie listening in vain for the owls
that used to summon the summer darkness.

The night air has fallen silent
like my Taishanese tongue that never speaks
since my parents are a decade gone and no-one
calls me by my name - *Yin*, their *Little Swallow*.

And where *are* those calligraphers of the sky?
I look up.
       In our eaves, only crumbling mud cups.

Crocuses, etc.
Elizabeth Gibson

Tonight, the wind is no longer pain-cold-full-of-grit,
but is instead a tongue, a vast creature greeting us,
curling and testing. It is still more cold than warm,
but it is soft, organic, spongey, a togetherness.
There is the quick smell of air-dry clay from the soil
in the holly borders—for one step—then gone,
but you grin. Spring is scattering its first specks
of warm, of welcome, checking we are ready
with books to read in parks, and denim jackets,
and people to walk and talk with, wind-tongue
shepherding us along, then squeezing us up to pause
by the canalside, briefly tight as crocuses,
our saffron red and sparking. I see the purple to come,
the viaduct, its rust-dripping arches, the stacking
of warehouses, pubs, woods, what is left and precious.
Do I see you, ahead? I have room for this one hug.
Maybe there can be nothing bigger. A hug is the pinnacle
of being—for me, anyway, precious in its scarcity
as strands of spice rattling in a little glass jar.
Maybe I should ask you, tease at that sliver of red
in a purple scarf and coat, keep my heart petals open.

Songbird Without Song
Isabelle Wei (15)

& without breath. Undress, in stillness, the red
-purply skirts of falling plums, their dusty skins
      burning   a carnal gem-mauve flushed
by dusk. Above:
            juncos & nightingales   circling air,
circling sky. Watch them swell from tree throats: nippy,
nipping at roots, hauling away   song
    & emblem. To the left, the bird tree is in full bloom
and is scattering wings, wheedlingly.
         See—   flocks of velvet, drifting
in the breeze. Humming. Thrumming.   Then:
    line of wind —greenish, clam-rimmed—
richly quiet. The thrushes vanish. The warblers. The whir
-ring: birds tossed beyond the O of *globe*, like a wreath
ringing ec*ology* (which breathes *oh, oh,* as in *look:*
songs of oiled wood—smooth & moonlit)—
      only now they've disappeared. There's no *o*
in that, in disappear. Only dis. Only sap. Only pear.
Remember this: yellow-bellied sapsuckers, humming
-birds sipping pears. Pearly.   The trees are quiet now,
their fruit untouched. Gone are the carols, the seed-strewn
    droppings, the whistling sunbirds—pollinating.
Both nature and literature are in mourning (look: it's wintry)
In the morning, nothing sings, the spun-out runner shining
softly, amber. Day's sole sound: footsteps down a hallway,
as though treading the woods, the leafy carpets, slinking
behind shadow-light.   In the afternoon:
    terms have disappeared. Are still disappearing.

Four so far—this, sap, pear, ring. Another three: birds, song,
humming. Another: thrumming.   See—
entire pages shattering. Like glass. Like church bells.
That's another one: bells. Bluebells. Bellbirds.
Snap the alliterative b's to leave: ellirds. Ridlles.
Never again will there b a raven (upon a midnight dreary),
nor a crane nor a cuckoo   clock: classic, pendulum
-clucked. Prettily beaks snap   like bands, like
      breath   bottled in bodies of nuthatches,
honeycreepers. Like a tinkerer's conceit—both puffed
up & primely witty—   stoppered. Gaze at these shiny
metaphors, sweet nest of a nest: migratory tweets darting
wing to wing. Down the hall, rattle off dishes: goose &
quail eggs & turkey & buffalo wings & chicken & chicken
wings & grouse & partridges & chicken & chicken
& chicken. Such bird-like names: caged, then forgotten.
Forgotten is the phrase: *cluck my tongue*. Forgotten
is the word: *bird*.   Other forgotten things: thanksgiving,
wintertide. Aerial migration. Hot chocolate.
Remembered things—or rather, *the present*:   hot
dawn. Hot eve—   Not Dawn & Eve but dawn & eve
as in: it's hot. Across the room, watch a woman with thin
lips rasp up music, dress it in wings of newsprint
ripped from the heap of papers at her feet. Watch her line
these slim parcels in ordered queues as though plopping
down a sound stall   (like Ursula, hawking
her wares)   & remember: markets swarmed
      with birds. Pigeons. Emus. & that word again:
chicken. Sound slips off tongues.   Silkily.
Another disappearance: feathered. Twitter. Chicken
& *song*.   Now we sell sound instead of—

Sickness in a Cool, Coastal Wood
Dominic Anaya Gulaya (16)

    1981
Mourning doves, escaping a hunt, are pulled
into the inviting glow of a slow wood full with fungi
bursting from and among rotting logs like seams.
A gentle transition, now: in-between bustling, is
entirely self contained. New rain falls, soaks,
and dries with sweltering noon. Mayflies live
half their lives in a single day's liminal hours.
In this mo(u)rning time, many sad men kiss
each other's bodies like they'll die tomorrow.
We think they drop like mayflies, but really,
their deaths are slow: all an unkept wood.
Hearts are left unfed, pumping weakly, and weary.
The earth bruises like a past-ripe peach, filling
with young bodies. When will it be sewn up tight?
The fungi crack softened logs wide open, and
their fuzziness grows across fresh graves,
covering them over many liminal mornings.

On the rocks
Corinna Broad

Staring into my drink, I see
a miniature Arctic.

The ice cube is a glacier
somewhere in Svalbard;

majestic, melting
at the rate of knots.

I spot a tiny polar bear
drifting on a raft of ice,

the water is curaçao blue.
As the glass warms in my hands,

the ice cube-glacier dwindles
then calves, sending a frothy

tsunami of alcohol and slimline
tonic across the surface.

I watch them disappear: glacier, ice,
tiny bear. I exhale cumulus clouds

of carbon, my face looms
above the meltwater like a sun.

Calima
Isabella Mead

arrives as young people leave; late summer,
as sunlight deepens, as August tips
into September. One afternoon, perhaps,

in a white town niched in a shadowed sierra,
a page of a newspaper stirs on a lounge-chair,
a moon-lizard pauses on the walls of a kitchen,

as golden sand-winds from the Sahara
return full swell to Andalusia,
to Al Andalus, to traces of home.

The moon-lizard bolts. The chair upturns.
The cobbled alleyways and tightknit streets
and winding walls and roof-terraces

blush with a film of russet-brown dust,
whitewash tempered to terracotta:
a diffusion of old desiccated blood.

The houses give little. They have only two words,
chaperoned across distances by sabulous air
to rusted signage lodged in glassless windows:

se vende   *se vende*   *se vende*[1]

---

[1] For sale

Fruit pickers, south of Rome
Caroline Maldonado

These days the sun's fierce
all records broken.
Figs discharge their sweetness,
the heart of them drunk with hornets,
shrivelled grapes hang like dark ribbons,
olive trees are barren.
Next year there'll be shortages.

These are days of thirst.
Days for the cool relief
of watermelons in la Pontina
where tourists seek secluded beaches
and Indian workers lift
the heavy globes under the sun.

Some die in the fields,
some on the road, others
on a mattress in a shared shack.
After 30 years of labour Kamal
picked up his last watermelon and fell.

With no family here who knows
where to send his body home?

Emergency Oxygen
Agata Maslowska

The flying fish like birds
glide in the air
aerodynamic bodies
with no scales

My body is flying inside
Boeing 737-800, made of
aluminium, zinc, magnesium,
copper, plastic, leather

My heart is soft:
oxygen, carbon,
hydrogen, nitrogen,
calcium, phosphorus

Inside my and the fish's gut
microplastics gather like
non-compostable dust

A cup, a bottle, a carrier
bag, a fork, a plate,
a bracelet, kite string

The flying fish and I
will decompose sooner
than the plastic debris,
than the body of the plane
in the ocean

Even the emergency oxygen
falling from the panels
above our heads
won't make us last

We rise in the air
in protest

Our hearts soft,
we rise in protest

On Precipitation
Ger Duffy

```
how      dark      light      the          clouds            rain
     how      down       windowpanes
        down        gutters        the         drains
          how    steadily      rain              streams
how      each   drop      falls    explodes    runs     on
              or       is      absorbed
     becomes           something              else
                stone      tree       sea
```

  air

                                                                                           cloud

           becomes   that   thing   only

   to   lift   again   to   disappear

                       might   rise   high   as

       or   might   become   cloud

                   might   we   observe   its

might   we   become   one   with   earth

       might   we   become   tree   stone

                as   useful   as   weeds   sea

                         nothing   more

THE POETS

Corinna Board teaches English as an additional language in Oxford. She grew up on a farm, and her writing is often inspired by the rural environment. She particularly enjoys exploring our connection to the more-than-human. *Arboreal*, her debut pamphlet, was published in January by The Black Cat Poetry Press. She tweets @corinnaboard and can also be found on Instagram @parole_de_reveuse.

Hannah Burrows is a genderqueer lesbian poet, facilitator and museum worker based in Birmingham, UK. They were commended in last year's VERVE poetry competition on the theme of protest. Their work has been featured online and in print by VERVE, English Heritage, Olney Magazine, Young Poets Network and others. They were a member of Birmingham University's winning UniSlam team in 2022, and have featured at poetry nights and a Sofar Sounds concert. They are a member of the VERVE Poetry Collective 2023-24. They are happiest near water.

Ger Duffy's poetry has been published by *PNR, Poetry Ireland Review, Under the Radar, The Ekphrastic Review* and other literary magazines. She is a Pushcart nominee. She has been awarded two poetry mentoring awards. Her poems have been anthologized in *Local Wonders, Washing Windows 111, In the Gold of the Flesh, The Stony Thursday Book*. Her poems have been placed or commended in the following competitions: Goldsmiths International, Travels with Joyce, Write by the Sea, The Francis Ledwidge Awards, The Allingham. She was a selected poet to read at the launch of *On Being* with Padraig O Tuama at the Southbank.

Lily Dyu is a Wales-based author and poet of Chinese descent. She's written four children's books and two outdoor guides, three of which were shortlisted for awards. Her poetry explores themes of nature and place, cultural hybridity, and how we find home and belonging. When she's not at her desk, you'll find her drifting in the woods or exploring lumpy places.

Elizabeth Gibson is a queer, neurodivergent poet and performer from Wigan, living in Manchester, who has been the recipient of a New North Poets Prize at the Northern Writers' Awards and a Developing Your Creative Practice Grant from Arts Council England. Elizabeth has had poems published in *Abridged, Atrium, Butcher's Dog, Confingo, Lighthouse,*

Magma, The North, Popshot, Spelt, Strix, Under the Radar, and anthologies from The Poetry Business and The Poetry School. Elizabeth has been commissioned by Manchester Poetry Library, Manchester Literature Festival, Manchester Pride, The Portico Library, Oldham Coliseum, Islington Mill, and Yorkshire Dance. https://elizabeth-gibson.com Twitter/Instagram: @Grizonne.

Dominic Anaya Gulaya (she/him) is a sixteen-year-old QTPOC and Disabled writer from Los Angeles. He studies creative writing at school, edits for and is on the Junior Board of Polyphony Lit, acts as a writer in residence at Collections of Transience, and is incredibly passionate about prison & police abolition, restorative justice, volunteering, and mutual aid. He also enjoys bass guitar, going to punk shows, horror movies, zines, computer science, and journalism! More of his work (and life) can be found on Instagram @desertfirelight.

Japmeh Kaur Gujral is 12 years old, lives in Birmingham and attends King Edwards High School for girls. 'Writing has always been an important part of my life. I started writing fiction stories and then developed a love for poetry. I feel that writing helps me explore my thoughts on different topics and put my opinions out there, hopefully along with sending a message close to my heart. In addition to writing, I love playing hockey, playing the harp and singing. I hope I get the opportunity to write many more poems and share my thoughts and feelings with the world.'

Roger Hare is Hertforshire-based and writes from things overheard, observed, and the stimulus offered by works of art. Currently without a pamphlet/collection, he has been anthologised and published many times in online/in-print journals, been a prize-winner/commended in several competitions and is Best-of-the-Net and Pushcart nominated. In 2023 he was supported by an Arts Council DYCP grant. He is found on twitter @RogerHare6

Emily Hunt is a 17-year-old writer from Warwickshire. She won her first award aged 13 for Best Nature Poem in the Betjeman Poetry Prize. Since then, she hasn't stopped writing. Nature and the environment is Emily's passion, and her writing reflects this. She has won many awards for her poetry, her most notable being First Place in the Guernsey Literary Festival 2021 and 2022 (Youth Category), First Place in the Stratford Literary Festival 2022 (Youth Category), First Place in the Young Wild

Writer Prize 2022, and First Place in the Solstice Prize for Young Writers 2021. Emily was awarded the title of Warwickshire Young Poet Laureate 2023 and spent a year as the Laureate performing at events, working with young people and writing commissioned pieces. During this time, she also ran her first workshop with The Wildlife Trust and judged the South Warwickshire Literary Festival's Poetry Competition. Her laureateship took her to some amazing venues, including the Birmingham Hippodrome, the RSC The Other Place, Compton Verney, and even a pop-up stage in the centre of Coventry. Find Emily on Instagram @ em_loves_nature_ or Twitter @em_nature.

Tim Kiely is a criminal barrister and writer based in East London. He is the author of three poetry pamphlets: *Hymn to the Smoke* (published by Indigo Dreams); *Plaque for the Unknown Socialist* (Back Room Poetry); and *No Other Life* (VOLE Books). He is a member of 'Poetry on the Picket Line', an occasional contributor to the work of the 'Poets Versus' collective and 'Poets for the Planet' and an active member of the Green Party of England and Wales. Follow him @TimKiely1 on most platforms and buy his books at timkielybooks.bigcartel.com

Kai Lee is a poet and dabbler in the liberal arts from Troy, Michigan who is currently living in Shanghai. China. She is 14 years old and has an optimistic viewpoint on life, always knowing that things will turn out for the better. She is incredibly thankful for her friends and family, who support her even though poetry is a tough talent to show off to the world. She wants to spread the message that no matter what your talent may be, whether it is basket-weaving or cardiology, make sure you cherish it and let it grow.

Caroline Maldonado's publications include translations from Italian, her own poetry, and sometimes a mix of the two. Five collections in translation have been published by Smokestack Books (2013-2022). *Isabella* was listed one of The Morning Star's Best Collections (2019) and her translation *Liminal* won a PEN Translates Award (2019). For seven years she chaired the Board of Trustees of the journal, Modern Poetry in Translation. A collection of her own poems *Faultlines* (Vole Books, 2022) includes a sequence responding to the actual and metaphorical (political, ecological) resonances of the 2016 earthquake in Le Marche where she lives part-time.

Agata Maslowska is a poet, writer, and translator born in Poland and living in Scotland. Her poetry and fiction have appeared in various magazines, including *Edinburgh Review, New Writing Scotland, Gutter, Magma, Blackbox Manifold, Interpreter's House, amberflora, Propel, Wet Grain*, and in several anthologies, including *Glasgow* (Dostoyevsky Wannabe, 2022) and *Footprints: Ecopoetry Anthology* (Broken Sleep Books, 2022). She is the recipient of the Scottish Book Trust New Writers Award, the Hawthornden Writing Fellowship, and the Gillian Purvis Award for New Writing. Her poetry submission received special commendation in the Oxford Brookes International Poetry Competition 2022. Website: https://agatamaslowska.co.uk

Isabella Mead's writing focuses on responses to place, particularly in terms of physical landscape as a metaphor for socio-political context. Her debut pamphlet *Dear Rwanda*, published in 2023 by Live Canon, is informed by two years spent living in a rural community of Rwanda as a volunteer. Her work has appeared in *Magma, Mslexia, The Telegraph, Poetry Wales, Anacapa Review* and *Poetry News*. She has won 8 poetry competitions, including the Julian Lennon Poetry Prize 2021. She specialises in learning and engagement in literary museums, is a Trustee of Jane Austen House, and enjoys being owned by a cat.

Lilly Prince is 15 and is currently studying at Bishop Perowne C of E college. 'I'm always doing something as I'm a dancer and involved in scouting which is a huge influence in my life since I have been very young. I started writing poetry over a year ago for school, but I have recently been writing a greater amount with the majority influenced by nature. I wrote this poem about climate change for a simple school competition, but I didn't know it was me so much; I'm truly grateful. This poem highlights all the problems that have occurred because of human's actions; from the biggest to the smallest issues. As a collective we need to change, after all we only have one life and one earth. Even the tiniest actions are creating the biggest differences...
So, switch off all lights when you're not in the room or plant a tree or two if the opportunity arises, I hope for big change for our world and I'm extremely thankful for this opportunity.'

Lesley Quayle is a poet, editor and folk/blues singer. Her work has appeared widely in magazines and journals. She has won a number of prizes and been nominated for a Forward award. Her latest collection is *The Invisible Woman* (Yaffle).

Disha Ramesh is 12 years old, currently in year 8 at King Edwards High School For Girls (KEHS). 'My favourite past times, until now, was anything to do with art and swimming. I recently discovered the amazing world of poetry and ever since, I have fallen in love with it. I never could have dreamt of being selected for this wonderful competition. Poetry has changed me for the better and I thank you VERVE Poetry Festival for giving me this opportunity.'

Aneesha Sandhu goes to King Edward VI High School for Girls and is currently 13. 'I live with my parents and younger sister. My family are a big part of my life, and they help inspire me to be the best I can be. They are one of the reasons I started writing in the first place. I really enjoy poetry. I love writing and feeling. Poetry is a big part of my self-expression. I also really enjoy playing the sport Squash. I'm quite an extroverted person who loves to meet new people and share my work.'

Tom Sastry grew up in Buckinghamshire and has lived in Bristol since 1999. After being chosen by Carol Ann Duffy as one of the 2016 Laureate's Choice poets, his debut pamphlet *Complicity* (2016) was a Poetry School Book of the Year and a Poetry Book Society pamphlet choice. Since then, he has published two collections, both with Nine Arches Press: *A Man's House Catches Fire* in 2019, which was highly commended in the Forward Prize and shortlisted for the Seamus Heaney First Collection Prize, and his latest book, *You have no normal country to return to* (2023).

Rachit Sharma lives in Noida, India, and is the founder and curator of Dillipoetry, a literary platform known for its experiential poetry workshops and forest healing walks. He is also part of the core team at Youth Alliance, where he designs and facilitates transformational journeys of (un) learning, healing, and enquiry in the youth leadership development domain. His poetry and other writings have been published by 20+ literary platforms and anthologies including - *Muse India, Livewire, The Indian Review, The Honest Ulsterman, SIMS Library of Poetry, California, The Logical Indian, The Quint* among others.

Harry Slater is a writer who lives on a flood plain in the East Midlands. He grew up in a forgotten corner of Yorkshire that's falling into the sea. He has an MA in English and Creative Writing, and has had poems and short stories published in *Dream Catcher* and *New Maps*.

Sue Spiers lives in Hampshire and works with Winchester Poetry Festival. Sue edits the annual anthology for the Open University Poetry Society and supports Winchester Muse, T'Articulation and Pens of the Earth groups. Her poems have appeared in *Acumen, Artemis, Dream Catcher, Fenland Poetry Journal, The North, Obsessed With Pipework, Prole, South* magazines and on-line at *Dust, Flight of the Dragonfly, The High Window, Ink, Sweat & Tears, The Lake* and *London Grip*. Her latest collection is *De Do Do Do, De Da Da Da* at Lulu.com. Sue Tweets @spiropoetry.

Alison Tanik is a Midlands-based poet, performer and playwright, currently studying for an MA in creative writing (poetry) at Manchester Metropolitan University. Under her stage name of 'Who the f*** is Alice', Alison headlines at poetry events around the country, performing erotic poetry as a means of questioning gender stereotypes and gender power imbalance. Alison also writes poetry of place, focusing her writing on Mesopotamia, Ireland and Scotland. Alison was an Associate Poet for the Derby Poetry Festival 2023.

Isabelle Wei is a fifteen-year-old poet and artist based in Hong Kong. She is the recipient of the 2023 Yamabuki Prize and has been recognised by the Wilbur and Niso Smith Foundation and the John Locke Institute. Recent publications include *Carolina Muse, IAMB,* and *Occulum*, among others. In her spare time, she enjoys writing and reading stories that reflect her love for the natural world.

Evie Williams is 11 and attends high school in Worcestershire. She enjoys dancing and takes part in regular theatre shows, alongside lifeguard training and surfing. Evie cares deeply about the environment and wants to make a difference to the world we live in. She lives with her mum, dad and cat, and can always be found listening to music and singing.

Milena Williamson is from Swarthmore, Pennsylvania and has lived in Belfast since 2017. She has a PhD in poetry from the Seamus Heaney Centre at Queen's University Belfast. A recipient of the Eric Gregory Award, she published her debut pamphlet *Charm for Catching a Train* in 2022 from Green Bottle Press. In 2024, her debut poetry collection *Into the Night that Flies So Fast* was published with Dedalus Press.

Laurie Wiseman is 12 years old and from London. His poetry been shortlisted in competitions including the Ledbury, and he was runner up in the Wicked Young Writers award. His passions include cricket, cricket and cricket

ABOUT VERVE POETRY PRESS

Verve Poetry Press is an award-winning press that focused initially on meeting a local need in Birmingham - a need for the vibrant poetry scene here in Brum to find a way to present itself to the poetry world via publication. Co-founded by Stuart Bartholomew and Amerah Saleh, it now publishes poets from all corners of the UK and beyond - poets that speak to the city's varied and energetic qualities and will contribute to its many poetic stories.

Added to this is a colourful pamphlet series, many featuring poets who have performed at our sister festival - and a poetry show series which captures the magic of longer poetry performance pieces by festival alumni such as Polarbear, Matt Abbott and Imogen Stirling.

The press has been voted Most Innovative Publisher at the Saboteur Awards, and has won the Publisher's Award for Poetry Pamphlets at the Michael Marks Awards.

Like the festival, we strive to think about poetry in inclusive ways and embrace the multiplicity of approaches towards this glorious art.

www.vervepoetrypress.com
@VervePoetryPres
mail@vervepoetrypress.com